POCKET
HAVAMAL™

OLIVE BRAY TRANSLATION

Edited & Designed by: Carrie Overton

Pocket Havamal

Olive Bray Translation

1st Edition ©2016 Carrie Overton

ISBN: 978-1-937571-28-3

We would like to give a hearty Hail to folk like you who made the Pocket Havamal series a best seller and thank you for supporting our Heathen family.

Many Blessings,
Carrie Overton
Huginnn & Muninn Publishing

For information on Asatru, Odinism and Germanic Heathenry please visit our website:

huginnandmuninn.net

Hail the Aesir!
Hail the Vanir!
Hail the Folk!

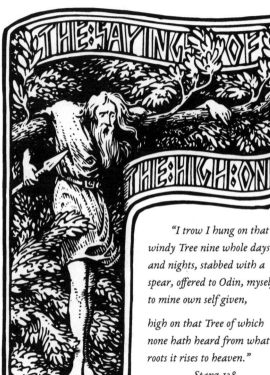

THE SAYINGS OF THE HIGH ONE

"I trow I hung on that windy Tree nine whole days and nights, stabbed with a spear, offered to Odin, myself to mine own self given,

high on that Tree of which none hath heard from what roots it rises to heaven."

Stanz 138

Odin by: W.G. Collingwood

HAVAMAL

ᚺᚨᚠᚠᛗᚨᚠᛚ

Wisdom for Wanderers and Counsel to Guests

1. At every door-way, ere one enters,
   one should spy round, one should
   pry round, for uncertain is the wit-
   ting that there be no foeman sitting,
   within, before one on the floor.

2. Hail, ye Givers! a guest is come; say!
   where shall he sit within? Much
   pressed is he who fain on the hearth
   would seek for warmth and weal.

3. He hath need of fire, who now is
   come, numbed with cold to the knee;
   food and clothing the wanderer craves
   who has fared o'er the rimy fell.

4. He craves for water, who comes for
   refreshment, drying and friendly bid-
   ding, marks of good will, fair fame if
   'tis won, and welcome once and again.

5. He hath need of his wits who wanders
   wide, aught simple will serve at home;
   but a gazing-stock is the fool who sits
   mid the wise, and nothing knows.

6. Let no man glory in the greatness of
   his mind, but rather keep watch o'er
   his wits. Cautious and silent let him
   enter a dwelling; to the heedful comes
   seldom harm, for none can find a
   more faithful friend than his wealth
   of mother wit.

7. Let the wary stranger who seeks refreshment keep silent with sharpened
   hearing; with his ears let him listen,
   and look with his eyes; thus each wise
   man spies out the way.

8. Happy is he who wins for himself fair fame and kindly words; but uneasy is that which a man doth own while it lies in another's breast.

9. Happy is he who hath in himself praise and wisdom in life; for oft doth a man ill counsel get when 'tis born in another's breast.

10. A better burden can no man bear on the way than his mother wit: 'tis the refuge of the poor, and richer it seems than wealth in a world untried.

11. A better burden can no man bear on the way than his mother wit: and no worse provision can he carry with him than too deep a draught of ale.

12. Less good than they say for the sons
of men is the drinking oft of ale: for
the more they drink, the less can they
think and keep a watch o'er their wits.

13. A bird of Unmindfulness flutters o'er
ale feasts, wiling away men's wits: with
the feathers of that fowl I was fettered
once in the garths of Gunnlod below.

14. Drunk was I then, I was over drunk in
that crafty jotun's court. But best is an
ale feast when man is able to call back
his wits at once.

15. Silent and thoughtful and bold in
strife the prince's bairn should be.

16. Joyous and generous let each man
show him until he shall suffer death.

17. A coward believes he will ever live
if he keep him safe from strife: but
old age leaves him not long in peace
though spears may spare his life.

18. A fool will gape when he goes to a
friend, and mumble only, or mope;
but pass him the ale cup and all in
a moment the mind of that man is
shown.

19. He knows alone who has wandered
wide, and far has fared on the way,
what manner of mind a man doth
own who is wise of head and heart.

20. Keep not the mead cup but drink thy
measure; speak needful words or none:
none shall upbraid thee for lack of
breeding if soon thou seek'st thy rest.

21. A greedy man, if he be not mindful,
    eats to his own life's hurt: oft the belly
    of the fool will bring him to scorn
    when he seeks the circle of the wise.

22. Herds know the hour of their going
    home and turn them again from the
    grass; but never is found a foolish
    man who knows the measure of his
    maw.

23. The miserable man and evil minded
    makes of all things mockery, and
    knows not that which he best should
    know, that he is not free from faults.

24. The unwise man is awake all night,
    and ponders everything over; when
    morning comes he is weary in mind,
    and all is a burden as ever.

25. The unwise man weens all who smile
and flatter him are his friends, nor
notes how oft they speak him ill when
he sits in the circle of the wise.

26. The unwise man weens all who smile
and flatter him are his friends; but
when he shall come into court he
shall find there are few to defend his
cause.

27. The unwise man thinks all to know,
while he sits in a sheltered nook; but
he knows not one thing, what he shall
answer, if men shall put him to proof.

28. For the unwise man 'tis best to be
mute when he comes amid the crowd,
for none is aware of his lack of wit
if he wastes not too many words; for
he who lacks wit shall never learn
though his words flow ne'er so fast.

29. Wise he is deemed who can question
    well, and also answer back: the sons of
    men can no secret make of the tidings
    told in their midst.

30. Too many unstable words are spoken
    by him who ne'er holds his peace; the
    hasty tongue sings its own mishap if it
    be not bridled in.

31. Let no man be held as a laugh-
    ing-stock, though he come as guest
    for a meal: wise enough seem many
    while they sit dry-skinned and are not
    put to proof.

32. A guest thinks him witty who mocks
    at a guest and runs from his wrath
    away; but none can be sure who
    jests at a meal that he makes not fun
    among foes.

33. Oft, though their hearts lean towards one another, friends are divided at table; ever the source of strife 'twill be, that guest will anger guest.

34. A man should take always his meals betimes unless he visit a friend, or he sits and mopes, and half famished seems, and can ask or answer nought.

35. Long is the round to a false friend leading, e'en if he dwell on the way; but though far off fared, to a faithful friend straight are the roads and short.

36. A guest must depart again on his way, nor stay in the same place ever; if he bide too long on another's bench the loved one soon becomes loathed.

37. One's own house is best, though
    small it may be; each man is master at
    home; though he have but two goats
    and a bark-thatched hut 'tis better
    than craving a boon.

38. One's own house is best, though
    small it may be, each man is master at
    home; with a bleeding heart will he
    beg, who must, his meat at every meal.

39. Let a man never stir on his road a step
    without his weapons of war; for unsure
    is the knowing when need shall arise
    of a spear on the way without.

40. I found none so noble or free with his
    food, who was not gladdened with
    a gift, nor one who gave of his gifts
    such store but he loved reward, could
    he win it.

41. Let no man stint him and suffer need
of the wealth he has won in life; oft is
saved for a foe what was meant for a
friend, and much goes worse than one
weens.

42. With raiment and arms shall friends
gladden each other, so has one proved
oneself; for friends last longest, if fate
be fair, who give and give again.

43. To his friend a man should bear him
as friend, and gift for gift bestow,
laughter for laughter let him ex-
change, but leasing pay for a lie.

44. To his friend a man should bear him
as friend, to him and a friend of his;
but let him beware that he be not the
friend of one who is friend to his foe.

45. Hast thou a friend whom thou trustest
well, from whom thou cravest good?
Share thy mind with him, gifts ex-
change with him, fare to find him oft.

46. But hast thou one whom thou trustest
ill yet from whom thou cravest good?
Thou shalt speak him fair, but falsely
think, and leasing pay for a lie.

47. Yet further of him whom thou trusted
ill, and whose mind thou dost misdoubt; thou shalt laugh with him but
withhold thy thought, for gift with
like gift should be paid.

48. Young was I once, I walked alone, and
bewildered seemed in the way; then I
found me another and rich I thought
me, for man is the joy of man.

49. Most blest is he who lives free and bold and nurses never a grief, for the fearful man is dismayed by aught, and the mean one mourns over giving.

50. My garments once I gave in the field to two land-marks made as men; heroes they seemed when once they were clothed; 'tis the naked who suffer shame!

51. The pine tree wastes which is perched on the hill, nor bark nor needles shelter it; such is the man whom none doth love; for what should he longer live?

52. Fiercer than fire among ill friends for five days love will burn; but anon 'tis quenched, when the sixth day comes, and all friendship soon is spoiled.

53. Not great things alone must one give
to another, praise oft is earned for
nought; with half a loaf and a tilted
bowl I have found me many a friend.

54. Little the sand if little the seas, little
are minds of men, for ne'er in the
world were all equally wise, 'tis shared
by the fools and the sage.

55. Wise in measure let each man be; but
let him not wax too wise; for never
the happiest of men is he who knows
much of many things.

56. Wise in measure should each man be;
but let him not wax too wise; seldom
a heart will sing with joy if the owner
be all too wise.

57. Wise in measure should each man be,
but ne'er let him wax too wise: who
looks not forward to learn his fate
unburdened heart will bear.

58. Brand kindles from brand until it be
burned, spark is kindled from spark,
man unfolds him by speech with man,
but grows over secret through silence.

59. He must rise betimes who fain of
another or life or wealth would win;
scarce falls the prey to sleeping wolves,
or to slumberers victory in strife.

60. He must rise betimes who hath few
to serve him, and see to his work
himself; who sleeps at morning is
hindered much, to the keen is wealth
half-won.

61. Of dry logs saved and roof-bark stored
    a man can know the measure, of fire-
    wood too which should last him out
    quarter and half years to come.

62. Fed and washed should one ride to
    court though in garments none too
    new; thou shalt not shame thee for
    shoes or breeks, nor yet for a sorry
    steed.

63. Like an eagle swooping over old
    ocean, snatching after his prey, so
    comes a man into court who finds
    there are few to defend his cause.

64. Each man who is wise and would wise
    be called must ask and answer aright.
    Let one know thy secret, but never
    a second, if three a thousand shall
    know.

65. A wise counselled man will be mild in
bearing and use his might in measure, lest when he come his fierce foes
among he find others fiercer than he.

66. Each man should be watchful and
wary in speech, and slow to put faith
in a friend. For the words which one
to another speaks he may win reward
of ill.

67. At many a feast I was far too late, and
much too soon at some; drunk was the
ale or yet unserved: never hits he the
joint who is hated.

68. Here and there to a home I had haply
been asked had I needed no meat
at my meals, or were two hams left
hanging in the house of that friend
where I had partaken of one.

69. Most dear is fire to the sons of men,
    most sweet the sight of the sun; good
    is health if one can but keep it, and to
    live a life without shame.

70. Not reft of all is he who is ill, for some
    are blest in their bairns, some in their
    kin and some in their wealth, and
    some in working well.

71. More blest are the living than the
    lifeless, 'tis the living who comes by
    the cow; I saw the hearth-fire burn in
    the rich man's hall and himself lying
    dead at the door.

72. The lame can ride horse, the handless
    drive cattle, the deaf one can fight and
    prevail, 'tis happier for the blind than
    for him on the bale-fire, for no man
    hath care for a corpse.

73. Best have a son though he be late born
    and before him the father be dead:
    seldom are stones on the wayside
    raised save by kinsmen to kinsmen.

74. Two are hosts against one, the tongue
    is the head's bane, 'neath a rough hide
    a hand may be hid; he is glad at night
    fall who knows of his lodging, short
    is the ship's berth, and changeful the
    autumn night, much veers the wind
    ere the fifth day and blows round yet
    more in a month.

75. He that learns nought will never
    know how one is the fool of another,
    for if one be rich another is poor and
    for that should bear no blame.

76. Cattle die and kinsmen die, thyself
    too soon must die, but one thing nev-
    er, I ween, will die, fair fame of one
    who has earned.

77. Cattle die and kinsmen die, thyself
too soon must die, but one thing never, I ween, will die, the doom on each
one dead.

78. Full-stocked folds had the Fatling's
sons, who bear now a beggar's staff:
brief is wealth, as the winking of an
eye, most faithless ever of friends.

79. If haply a fool should find for himself
wealth or a woman's love, pride waxes
in him but wisdom never and onward
he fares in his folly.

80. All will prove true that thou askest
of runes, those that are come from
the gods, which the high Powers
wrought, and which Odin painted
then silence is surely best.

81. Praise day at even, a wife when dead,
a weapon when tried, a maid when
married, ice when 'tis crossed, and ale
when 'tis drunk.

82. Hew wood in wind, sail the seas in a
breeze, woo a maid in the dark, for
day's eyes are many, work a ship for
its gliding, a shield for its shelter, a
sword for its striking, a maid for her
kiss;

83. Drink ale by the fire, but slide on the
ice; buy a steed when 'tis lanky, feed
thy horse neath a roof, and thy hound
in the yard.

84. The speech of a maiden, should no
man trust, nor the words which a
woman says; for their hearts were
shaped on a whirling wheel and false-
hood fixed in their breasts.

85. Breaking bow, or flaring flame,
ravening wolf, or croaking raven,
routing swine, or rootless tree, waxing
wave, or seething cauldron,

86. flying arrows, or falling billow, ice of
a night time, coiling adder, woman's
bed-talk, or broken blade, play of
bears or a prince's child,

87. sickly calf or self-willed thrall, witches flattery, new-slain foe, brother's
slayer, though seen on the highway,
half burned house, or horse too swift,
useless were it with one leg broken, be
never so trustful as these to trust.

88. Let none put faith in the first sown
fruit nor yet in his son too soon;
whim rules the child and weather the
field, each is open to chance.

89. Like the love of women, whose
thoughts are lies, is the driving
un-roughshod, o'er slippery ice of a
two-year-old, ill-tamed and gay; or in
a wild wind steering a helmless ship,
or the lame catching reindeer in the
rime-thawed fell.

90. Now plainly I speak, since both I have
seen; unfaithful is man to maid; we
speak them fairest when thoughts are
falsest and wile the wisest of hearts.

91. Let him speak soft words and offer
wealth who longs for a woman's love,
praise the shape of the shining maid,
he wins who thus doth woo.

92. Never a whit should one blame another whom love hath brought into
bonds: oft a witching form will fetch
the wise which holds not the heart of
fools.

93. Never a whit should one blame another for a folly which many befalls; the might of love makes sons of men into fools who once were wise.

94. The mind knows alone what is nearest the heart, and sees where the soul is turned: no sickness seems to the wise so sore as in nought to know content.

95. This once I felt when I sat without in the reeds, and looked for my love; body and soul of me was that sweet maiden yet never I won her as wife.

96. Billing's daughter I found on her bed, fairer than sunlight sleeping, and the sweets of lordship seemed to me nought save I lived with that lovely form.

97. Yet nearer evening come thou, Odin,
    if thou wilt woo a maiden: all were
    undone save two knew alone such a
    secret deed of shame.'

98. So away I turned from my wise intent,
    and deemed my joy assured, for all her
    liking and all her love I weened that I
    yet should win.

99. When I came ere long the war troop
    bold were watching and waking all:
    with burning brands and torches
    borne they showed me my sorrowful
    way.

100. Yet nearer morning I went, once
     more, the housefolk slept in the hall,
     but soon I found a barking dog tied
     fast to that fair maid's couch.

101. Many a sweet maid when one knows
her mind is fickle found towards men:
I proved it well when that prudent lass
I sought to lead astray : shrewd maid,
she sought me with every insult and I
won therewith no wife.

102. In thy home be joyous and generous
to guests discreet shalt thou be in
thy bearing, mindful and talkative,
wouldst thou gain wisdom oft making
mention of good. He is 'Simpleton'
named who has nought to say, for
such is the fashion of fools.

103. I sought that old Jotun, now safe am
I back, little served my silence there;
but whispering many soft speeches I
won my desire in Suttung's halls.

104. I bored me a road there with Rati's
tusk and made room to pass through
the rock; while the ways of the Jotuns
stretched over and under I dared my
life for a draught.

105. 'Twas Gunnlod who gave me on a
golden throne a draught of the glori-
ous mead but with poor reward did I
pay her back for her true and troubled
heart.

106. In a wily disguise I worked my will;
little is lacking to the wise for the
Soul-stirrer now, sweet Mead of Song
is brought to men's earthly abode.

107. I misdoubt me if ever again I had
come from the realms of the Jotun
race₃ had I not served me of Gunnlod,
sweet woman, Her whom I held in
mine arms.

108. Came forth, next day, the dread Frost
Giants, and entered the High One's
hall: they asked--was the Baleworker
back mid the powers, or had Suttung
slain him below?

109. A ring-oath Odin I trow had taken-
how shall one trust his troth? 'twas he
who stole the mead from Suttung, and
Gunnlod caused to weep.

110. 'Tis time to speak from the Sage's
Seat; hard by the Well of Weird I saw
and was silent, I saw and pondered, I
listened to the speech of men.

111. Of runes they spoke, and the read-
ing of runes was little withheld from
their lips: at the High One's hall, in
the High One's hall, I thus heard the
High One say:

112. I counsel thee, Stray-Singer, accept
my counsels, they will be thy boon if
thou obey'st them, they will work thy
weal if thou win'st them: rise never at
night time except thou art spying or
seekest a spot without.

113. I counsel thee, Stray-Singer, accept my
counsels, they will be thy boon if thou
obey'st them, they will work thy weal
if thou win'st them: thou shalt never
sleep in the arms of a sorceress, lest she
should lock thy limbs;

114. So shall she charm that thou shalt
not heed the council or words of the
king, nor care for thy food or the joys
of mankind, but fall into sorrowful
sleep.

115. I counsel thee, Stray-Singer, accept
my counsels, they will be thy boon if
thou obey'st them, they will work thy
weal if thou win'st them: seek not ever
to draw to thyself in love-whispering
another's wife.

116. I counsel thee, Stray-Singer, accept my
counsels, they will be thy boon if thou
obey'st them, they will work thy weal
if thou win'st them: should thou long
to fare over fell and firth provide thee
well with food.

117. I counsel thee, Stray-Singer, accept
my counsels, they will be thy boon if
thou obey'st them, they will work thy
weal if thou win'st them: tell not ever
an evil man if misfortunes thee be-
fall, from such ill friend thou needst
never seek return for thy trustful
mind.

118. Wounded to death, have I seen a man
by the words of an evil woman; a lying
tongue had bereft him of life, and all
without reason of right.

119. I counsel thee, Stray-Singer, accept
my counsels9 they will be thy boon if
thou obey'st them, they will work thy
weal if thou win'st them : hast thou a
friend whom thou trustest well, fare
thou to find him oft; for with brush-
wood grows and with grasses high the
path where no foot doth pass.

120. I counsel thee, Stray-Singer, accept my
counsels, they will be thy boon if thou
obey'st them, they will work thy weal
if thou win'st them: in sweet converse
call the righteous to thy side, learn a
healing song while thou livest.

121. I counsel thee, Stray-Singer, accept
my counsels, they will be thy boon if
thou obey'st them, they will work thy
weal if thou win'st them: be never the
first with friend of thine to break the
bond of fellowship; care shall gnaw
thy heart if thou canst not tell all thy
mind to another.

122. I counsel thee, Stray-Singer, accept my
counsels, they will be thy boon if thou
obey'st them, they will work thy weal
if thou win'st them: never in speech
with a foolish knave shouldst thou
waste a single word.

123. From the lips of such thou needst not
look for reward of thine own good
will; but a righteous man by praise
will render thee firm in favour and
love.

124. There is mingling in friendship when man can utter all his whole mind to another; there is nought so vile as a fickle tongue; no friend is he who but flatters.

125. I counsel thee, Stray-Singer, accept my counsels, they will be thy boon if thou obey'st them, they will work thy weal if thou win'st them: strive not in three words with a man worse than thee; oft the worst lays the best one low.

126. I counsel thee, Stray-Singer, accept my counsels, they will be thy boon if thou obey'st them, they will work thy weal if thou win'st them: be not a shoe-maker nor yet a shaft maker save for thyself alone: let the shoe be misshap-en, or crooked the shaft, and a curse on thy head will be called.

127. I counsel thee, Stray-Singer, accept my
counsels, they will be thy boon if thou
obey'st them, they will work thy weal
if thou win'st them: when in peril
thou seest thee, confess thee in peril
nor ever give peace to thy foes.

128. I counsel thee, Stray-Singer, accept my
counsels, they will be thy boon if thou
obey'st them, they will work thy weal
if thou win'st them: rejoice not ever at
tidings of ill, but glad let thy soul be
in good.

129. I counsel thee, Stray-Singer, accept my
counsels, they will be thy boon if thou
obey'st them : they will work thy weal
if thou win'st them: look not up in
battle when men are as beasts, lest the
wights bewitch thee with spells.

130. I counsel thee, Stray-Singer, accept my
counsels, they will be thy boon if thou
obey'st them, they will work thy weal
if thou win'st them: wouldst thou win
joy of a gentle maiden, and lure to
whispering of love, thou shalt make
fair promise, and let it be fast, none
will scorn their weal who can win it.

131. I counsel thee, Stray-Singer, accept my
counsels, they will be thy boon if thou
obey'st them, they will work thy weal
if thou win'st them: I pray thee be
wary, yet not too wary, be wariest of
all with ale, with another's wife, and
a third thing eke, that knaves outwit
thee never.

132. I counsel thee, Stray-Singer, accept
my counsels, they will be thy boon if
thou obey'st them, they will work thy
weal if thou win'st them: hold not in
scorn, nor mock in thy halls a guest or
wandering wight.

133. They know but unsurely who sit
within what manner of man is come:
none is found so good but some fault
attends him, or so ill but he serves for
somewhat.

134. I counsel thee, Stray-Singer, accept
my counsels, they will be thy boon if
thou obey'st them, they will work thy
weal if thou win'st them: hold never
in scorn the hoary singer; oft the
counsel of the old is good; come words
of wisdom from the withered lips of
him left to hang among hides, to rock
with the rennets and swing with the
skins.

135. I counsel thee, Stray-Singer, accept
my counsels, they will be thy boon if
thou obey'st them, they will work thy
weal if thou win'st them: growl not at
guests nor drive them from the gate
but show thyself gentle to the poor.

136. Mighty is the bar to be moved away
for the entering in of all. Shower thy
wealth, or men shall wish thee every
ill in thy limbs.

137. I counsel thee, Stray-Singer, accept my
counsels, they will be thy boon if thou
obey'st them, they will work thy weal
if thou win'st them: when ale thou
quaffest call upon earth's might-—
'tis earth drinks in the floods. [Earth
prevails o'er drink, but fire o'er sickness, the oak o'er binding, the earcorn
o'er witchcraft, the rye spur o'er rup-
ture, the moon o'er rages, herb o'er
cattle plagues, runes o'er harm.]

Odin's Quest after the Runes

138. I trow I hung on that windy Tree nine
     whole days and nights, stabbed with a
     spear, offered to Odin, myself to mine
     own self given, high on that Tree of
     which none hath heard from what
     roots it rises to heaven.

139. None refreshed me ever with food
     or drink, I peered right down in the
     deep; crying aloud I lifted the Runes,
     then back I fell from thence.

140. Nine mighty songs I learned from the
     great son of Bale-thorn, Bestla's sire;
     I drank a measure of the wondrous
     Mead, with the Soulstirrer's drops I
     was showered.

141. Ere long I bare fruit, and throve full well, I grew and waxed in wisdom; word following word, I found me words, deed following deed, I wrought deeds.

142. Hidden Runes shalt thou seek and interpreted signs, many symbols of might and power, by the great Singer painted, by the high Powers fashioned, graved by the Utterer of gods.

143. For gods graved Odin, for elves graved Da'i'n, Dvalin the Dallier for dwarfs, All-wise for Jotuns, and I, of myself, graved some for the sons of men.

144. Dost know how to write, dost know how to read, dost know how to paint, dost know how to ask, dost know how to send, dost know how to prove, dost know how to offer, dost know how to spend?

145. Better ask for too little than offer too much, like the gift should be the boon; better not to send than to overspend. Thus Odin graved ere the world began; then he rose from the deep, and came again.

146. Those songs I know, which nor sons of men nor queen in a king's court knows; the first is Help which will bring thee help in all woes and in sorrow and strife.

147. A second I know, which the son of men must sing, who would heal the sick.

148. A third I know: if sore need should come of a spell to stay my foes; when I sing that song, which shall blunt their swords, nor their weapons nor staves can wound.

149. A fourth I know: if men make fast in chains the joints of my limbs, when I sing that song which shall set me free, spring the fetters from hands and feet.

150. A fifth I know: when I see, by foes shot, speeding a shaft through the host, flies it never so strongly I still can stay it, if I get but a glimpse of its flight.

151. A sixth I know: when some thane would harm me in runes on a moist tree's root, on his head alone shall light the ills of the curse that he called upon mine.

152. A seventh I know: if I see a hall high o'er the bench-mates blazing, flame it ne'er so fiercely I still can save it, I know how to sing that song.

153. An eighth I know: which all can sing
for their weal if they learn it well;
Where hate shall wax 'mid the warrior
sons, I can calm it soon with that
song.

154. A ninth I know: when need befalls
me to save my vessel afloat, I hush the
wind on the stormy wave, and soothe
all the sea to rest.

155. A tenth I know: when at night the
witches ride and sport in the air, such
spells I weave that they wander home
out of skins and wits bewildered.

156. An eleventh I know: if haply I lead
my old comrades out to war, I sing
'neath the shields, and they fare forth
mightily safe into battle, safe out of
battle, and safe return from the strife.

157. A twelfth I know: if I see in a tree a
corpse from a halter hanging, such
spells I write, and paint in runes, that
the being descends and speaks.

158. A thirteenth I know: if the new-born
son of a warrior I sprinkle with water,
that youth will not fail when he fares
to war, never slain shall he bow before
sword.

159. A fourteenth I know: if I needs must
number the Powers to the people of
men, I know all the nature of gods
and of elves which none can know
untaught.

160. A fifteenth I know, which Folk-stirrer
sang, the dwarf, at the gates of Dawn;
he sang strength to the gods, and skill
to the elves, and wisdom to Odin who
utters.

161. A sixteenth I know: when all sweet-
     ness and love I would win from some
     artful wench, her heart I turn, and
     the whole mind change of that fair-
     armed lady I love.

162. A seventeenth I know: so that e'en the
     shy maiden is slow to shun my love.

163. These songs, Stray-Singer, which
     man's son knows not, long shalt thou
     lack in life, obey'st them, though thy
     weal if thou win'st them, thy boon if
     thou thy good if haply thou gain'st
     them.

164. An eighteenth I know: which I ne'er
     shall tell to maiden or wife of man,
     save alone to my sister, or haply to her
     who folds me fast in her arms; most
     safe are secrets known to but one--
     the songs are sung to an end.

165. Now the sayings of the High One
are uttered in the hall for the weal
of men, for the woe of jotuns, Hail,
thou who hast spoken! Hail, thou that
knowest! Hail, ye that have hear-
kened! Use, thou who hast learned!

TOTMS

ᛏᛟᛏᛗᛊ

TOTEMS

TOTMS

Made in the USA
Lexington, KY
09 December 2016